RE-CREATE

GROW , EVOLVE AND ADAPT

VAISHNAVI ROY

The pillar of my life, my dad who has always pushed me beyond my limits.

Contents

Preface

What can I do to change my identity? What can I do to better my current situation? How can I grow in the most efficient way? How can I emulate him/her?

Does any of this sound familiar?

We've all had this question, searched for answers to it numerous times, read many wonderful books, listened to countless amazing podcasts, movies, and motivating talks that inspire us, and what not just to find the answer "how do I change?"

But the key question here is, "Has anything changed?"

Change can be unsettling, but it is inevitable, just as the world and people around us change; it is unavoidable and as certain as day and night. The good news is that you have already taken this step, putting you ahead of half of the population. You can undoubtedly change if you think about it and take action in that direction.

Re-create is a book that will effectively change your perspective, help you with your personal development, and allow you to grow, evolve, and adapt.

Finally, this book is meant to broaden your perspective; it is not meant to "teach" or impart life lessons.

1

THE CORE

Knowing yourself is the beginning of all wisdom.
-Aristotle

IDENTITY

Specification, individuality, self, character, originality, distinctiveness, singularity, peculiarity, all of these words somewhere refer to the same meaning – identity.

"Identity refers to who or what a person or thing is.

Do you know yourself well enough now that you understand what identity is? Many questions are related to this, and I believe they will lead to a "conclusion" on how one can understand oneself and why it is so important in life.

So, how do we learn about our personalities and, more importantly, our potential?

The first step toward understanding yourself is to recognize that you don't know yourself well enough.

Self-awareness is essential for going through the transformational process and recognizing your ignorance of simply not knowing yourself; if you did know yourself, you would have been very disciplined; and would have to know everything before commuting any mistake but you are full of flaws; perhaps you don't know yourself as well as you think you do.

You can transform yourself into a different person by developing or creating an identity that connects who you are to who you are becoming with significant and long-term change.

When it comes to identity, the most important factor is how people perceive themselves in terms of relationships, careers, and employment. People's perceptions of their lives influence their perceptions of their identities.

What goes wrong every time you try to change your identity or recreate a product (you) that you already created?

By viewing yourself as a stranger, you can try to understand how that person's emotions work, how they behave around certain people, their highs and lows, what inspires them, and what distinguishes them from others.

And having such clarity about yourself, even if it is only 50%, will help a lot in knowing who you are and where you need to go.

CHANGE

You must recognize that we exist in two worlds: your inner and outer worlds. Your inner world is who you truly are, whereas your outer world is your surroundings. The main issue with people is that, even when their outer world changes, which it will, their inner world does not. To put it another way, "your desire and being are not in alignment."

As a result, when you try to change, you remain stuck in your reluctance and are unable to do so because the original you, your inner self, has not changed. Because you are forcing yourself to do something, the process becomes completely unnatural. However, because you are putting pressure on yourself and building up resistance, you will eventually revert to your previous course; this is why it feels so out of place, if not unnatural.

So how can we move from the unnatural to natural process?

Changing one's inner reality is a simple solution to this problem because it makes changes to the outside world appear more natural and the process appears simpler and effortless.

So, what exactly is expected?

Clarity - Clarity is essential because it helps you understand things better and gives you a sense of direction. Clarity is linked with thoughts; if you are clear in your thoughts, you will be able to create clear responses because clear thoughts create clear responses and unclear thoughts create unclear responses. Having clarity is preferable to aimlessly drifting without direction. However, when clarity dawns on us, which can be triggered by any book, talk, friend, or your introspection, it serves as a baseline from which to operate, unlocking your hidden potential.

But how do we gain clarity? The solution is simply to ask yourself these powerful questions.

a)What would you like to change?

b)What motivates you to change?

c)Why is this major shift significant?

d)What resources are available for it?

As you begin to gain clarity, you must understand that change is difficult. Because your brain has been trained to prefer familiarity, it will resist change, making it difficult and uncomfortable. No matter how welcome the change is, we will struggle to incorporate it into our lives.

Let us understand this: when we are born, our brain is malleable and we are constantly exposed to new experiences; we figure out what is good for survival and what is not. And because it becomes accustomed to doing certain things in a certain way over time, inducing change can be difficult. But how does the change happen? The change happens because of neuroplasticity, which is the brain's ability to modify, change, and adapt through life. However, once the brain accepts the change, it begins to make new sequences, patterns, and combinations, which begins the process of changing your mind.

1. Understand "IT'S OKAY TO FALL BACK "

As I previously stated, change is difficult, no matter how appealing it may appear. What do you do in these circumstances?

"Be prepared to re-diagnose the problem if the process appears to fail," in other words, make a mistake.

Falling back from the process, or making mistakes, is a foregone conclusion. However, if you think about it, this can be an excellent opportunity, because it will help us understand things in a better and deeper way.

when a product is being developed, it's tested, modified, and a few things are changed according to the requirement, similarly, when you are recreating yourself, there are a few things that are going to fall back, which you have to re-diagnose and correct it. mistakes help you explore alternatives, you get an opportunity to rethink, change your perspective, be more aware, think more creatively and this time, since you have had a setback, the solution is

3) HABIT - How will the brain development patterns and combinations? This will happen through habits.

This process of developing habits is divided into three steps:

a) Identify - it is critical to identify which habits you want to change. Say which aspect you want to change; because you already have clarity, this step will be easier, and you know yourself better than anyone else. Make a note of it. For example, you want to improve your speaking skills, or you want to get in shape, or you want to look a certain way, or you want to improve your personality; similarly, there may be several things you want to change, so you identify the habit.

b) Apply logic - why is applying logic beneficial? You are consciously aware of what, when, why, and how you apply logic to anything. So when you realize this is what I want to change, but why? How will it benefit you? It is also important to understand how the habit will help you become a better version of yourself, and how it will lay the groundwork for your life, because, at the end of the day, the habit is you, they are difficult to break because the brain will resist the change, but they will eventually set the tone for life.

a. Replace the habit - once you understand what habit you need to change and why you need to change it, replace the old habit with new ones. For example, if you want to build great speaking skills, you need to know what will help you do so. Learning a few words every day, recording, and listing to yourself will boost your confidence, and practice speaking to more and more people. Similarly, if a person wants to be a good athlete, they practice day and night. No one is born a certain way, so dedication is essential.

b) Repeat - For the brain to accept change and for it to feel normal and natural, you must repeat the process daily.

At first, you may feel tired and want to give up, but this is because you have been developing certain habits for years and things do not happen overnight. Tell me one thing; did you learn to write ABCD easily as a child? No, you practiced it every day until you could close your eyes and do it. Similarly, we must repeat the habits we have decided to change over and over again. Understand that reinvention is a practice, not a quick fix or an overnight solution.

2

FIND MEANING AND PURPOSE

We all want to find purpose, even if we don't know what it is. As nice as it sounds, it is not an easy process. We all have ideas about purpose in life, but sometimes these are based on ideas from community and families. The purpose of life appears to be to attain certain money or have certain status in society. If this gives you certain fulfilment, that's fine. All you need to know is that purpose needs to give you a certain fulfilment in life.

Ask yourself these questions as it is important which can lead to greater happiness and success in life. Purpose is like a fingerprint, unique.

A)Why are you looking for meaning in your life?

B) Why are you seeking purpose in your life?

C) What keeps you away from finding your purpose?

3

Clear clutter / Remove Negativity

We've all heard the term toxic, and we've all heard people tell us to avoid toxic or negative people because they drain us.

So, what exactly do you mean by toxicity? A toxic person is anyone whose behaviour adds negativity to your life, someone who brings out the worst in you, someone who drains the life out instead of filling it, such people can be both manipulative and abusive, someone who questions your own sanity and basically everything you have ever known, such people are negativity and drama to your life, bring out the demon in you.

what toxicity does to you ?

Toxicity in people isn't considered a mental disorder. But there could be underlying mental problems that cause someone to act in toxic ways, including a personality disorder.

Types

Friend from the Past: This is someone you've known for a long time. Maybe you went to elementary school together or were neighbours when you were younger. You are now feeling guilty about ending the relationship.

Friend by Vicinity: This is a person who comes with another person in your life. Perhaps it's your partner's best friend, your friend's brother, or your best friend's childhood friend. You feel bad because you don't want to put your significant other in an awkward situation.

Contextual friend: This is someone you see all the time in a specific area of your life-someone you work with every day... somebody from your flag football team... somebody who lives down the hall You feel bad brushing them aside because you see them all the time.

The 7 Types of Toxic People

Here are the 7 types of toxic people to watch out for:

1)The Narcissistic Conversationalist

Have you ever been having a conversation with someone who keeps interrupting you? Maybe I should rephrase that sentence: have you ever tried to talk to someone who won't let you? Conversational narcissists adore talking about themselves—or simply hearing themselves speak. They don't ask you any questions, don't wait for your responses, and won't stop talking. These people will become completely self-centered in a relationship and will never be attentive to your needs

The Strait Jacket

The straitjacket is someone who wants to control everything and everyone around them. They want to be in charge of what you do, what you say, and even what you think. You know the person I am talking about—they freak out when you disagree with them, and won't stop trying to convince you that they are right and you should do what they say. In a relationship, this person will give you no breathing room and will constantly nag you until you are in complete alignment with them. Be careful, these people will go after your emotional, conversational, and mental freedom until you have nothing left. Get out while you can!

2) Emotional Moocher

An emotional moocher is also known as a “spiritual vampire,” because they tend to suck the positivity out of you or bleed you emotionally dry. These are the people who always have something sad, negative, or pessimistic to say. In conversations and relationships, they can never see the positive, and tend to bring everyone down with them. If you’re with someone and they only have bad things to say whenever you see them, watch out; it might not get better.

4) The Drama Magnet

Some unpleasant people are drama magnets. There is always a problem. Always. Of course, as soon as one issue is resolved, a new one arises. And they don’t want your advice—just your pity, support, and empathy! They never appear to want to correct anything, despite your offers of assistance and ideas. Instead, they complain and complain. Drama magnets are victims in relationships and thrive during crises because it makes them feel important.

A person who shines a spotlight on adversity should be on guard since you might someday join in the drama.

3)The JJ

Those who are JJs are jealous-judgmental. We can recognise a JJ from a mile away, and I want to demonstrate to you how to do the same. Because they can’t be pleased for anyone else around them due to their extreme self-hatred, jealous people are extremely toxic. Additionally, their envy frequently manifests itself as judgement, criticism, or rumours. They believe that everyone else is terrible, uncool, or deficient in some way. You never know what someone is saying about you behind your back if they start to gossip enviously about other people. This person may be toxic.

5) The Fibber

Before I learnt about human lie detection, I had a lot of liars in my life. It is exhausting to be around pathological liars, fibbers, and exaggerators. It's hard to trust a liar in a relationship, regardless of how many little white lies or blatant big lies they say. Because we are always questioning their words, dishonesty drains us. Get out of there before you are misled to if your gut tells you something is off.

6) The Tank

Everything is crushed in a tank's wake. A human tank always has the upper hand, doesn't consider the opinions or sentiments of others, and prioritises themselves above all else. Tanks are extremely conceited and believe their personal thoughts to be absolute truths in a relationship. They perceive every interaction and person as a problem that needs to be overcome since they frequently believe that they are the smartest person in the room. When attempting to establish a loving connection, they hardly ever view others as equals, which can be difficult. Get out while you can if you feel like your opinions aren't being heard or that you aren't being respected.

How to Deal with Toxicity?

Did someone pop into your head as I explained these toxic personality types? If you have someone in your life whom you dread seeing, who doesn't respect your opinions, or who makes you feel bad about yourself in any way, then you need to just say no.

You have to keep saving and helping this person with their issues.

You feel depleted after being with them and are either concealing or covering up for them.

You become enraged, upset, or melancholy around them.

They make you slander or act cruelly

You believe you must win their favour.

You are impacted by their issues or drama

They disregard your needs and refuse to accept "no."

You deserve to surround yourself with amazing, encouraging, and kind people. In actuality, life is too short to waste time with those that hinder your ability to be your best selves. I'm hoping this essay will serve as your defence against toxic people.

4

Raise your self worth

What does the term "self worth" or "self esteem" mean to you? so how would you set a higher benchmark?

You've probably heard of the several "self" terms.

There are many different types of self-care, including self-love, self-compassion, self-acceptance, and self-respect.

There are numerous words that can be used to express how we think about, feel about, and behave toward ourselves. It's reasonable if they all start to seem the same to you, yet they are distinct ideas with their own interpretations, conclusions, and goals.

The Psychology of Self-Worth

The idea of self-worth may not be as frequently studied in psychology as self-esteem or self-confidence, but that doesn't make it any less significant. Self-worth is fundamental to who we are; our ideas, feelings, and behavior are all closely related to how we perceive our value and deservingness as people.

What Is the Self-Worth Theory?

According to the self-worth hypothesis, a person's top objective in life should be to obtain self-acceptance, and self-acceptance is frequently attained through success.

Success, on the other hand, is frequently found via rivalry with others.

Therefore, it follows logically that competing with others might give us the impression that we have accomplished a lot, which helps us feel proud of ourselves and improves our acceptance of ourselves.

The theory holds that there are four main elements of the self-worth model:

1. Ability;
2. Effort;
3. Performance;
4. Self-worth.

The first three interact with one another to influence how much one values themselves. Performance is largely influenced by one's aptitude and effort, and all three factors have a role in one's sense of value and worth.

Despite the fact that this theory offers a solid insight of how we often sense self-worth, it is sad that we place such a high value on our accomplishments. In addition to competing with and "winning" over others, there are a variety of additional elements that might influence how we feel about ourselves.

What Determines Self-Worth?

1. The self-worth idea states that our success in one or more activities we value and how we rate our own talents make up the majority of what makes us feel valued.
2. But most people gauge their own worth using different criteria. Here are the top five elements that people consider when assessing their own worth and that of

others:

3. Appearance—whether measured by the number on the scale, the size of clothing worn, or the kind of attention received by others;

4. Net worth, which can refer to earnings, tangible belongings, financial assets, or all three;

5. Who you know/your social circle—Some people assess their worth and that of others based on their position and the significant and powerful individuals they know;

6. What you do/your career—We frequently evaluate people based on their occupations; for instance, a stockbroker is frequently viewed as more successful and useful than a janitor or a teacher;

7. Your achievements – As previously said, we frequently consider someone's achievements when determining their worth (whether it be our own or another person's), such as financial success, SAT test scores, or other honours.

8. Your accomplishments—As mentioned earlier, we frequently use someone's accomplishments to assess their value (whether that value is our own or that of another person), such as business success, SAT test results, or placing in a marathon or other sports competition .

- Your to-do list: Reaching goals and checking items off your list are nice, but they don't directly correlate with how valuable you are as a person.
- • You do: What you choose to do is irrelevant. What important is that you perform it well and are satisfied by it;
- • The social media platforms you use: Furthermore, it is irrelevant how many people follow you on Twitter or retweet your tweets. Although it can be educational and

beneficial to take into account others' viewpoints, their ideas have no bearing on our inherent worth;

- Your age is: There is nothing you are too young or old for. Your age is only a number and has nothing to do with how valuable you are as a person.
- • Other people: As it was stated previously, it is irrelevant what other people believe or what they have done or achieved. What you believe, say, and do about yourself matters considerably more than what other people think, say, or do;

• The distance you can run: One of the least significant aspects of your self-worth is how fast you run a mile (or for anything else, for that matter). Congratulations if you enjoy running and find satisfaction in lowering your time! If not, congratulations! Your worth is not determined by your ability to run;

- Your grades: We all have different strengths and weaknesses, and some of us are simply not cut out for class. This has no bearing on our value as people, and a straight-A student is just as valuable and worthy as a straight-F student or a dropout;
- • The amount of friends you have: Your worth as a person has nothing to do with the number of connections or friends you have. What matters most is how well your connections turn out;

• Your relationship status: Whether you are single, dating someone casually, or in a serious relationship, your value remains unchanged. Your relationship status has nothing to do with your social circle or professional connections. What matters most is how well your connections turn out;

· Your relationship status: Whether you are single, dating casually, or in a committed relationship, your value is the same regardless of your relationship;

· Your preferences: Whether or not you have "excellent taste," whether or not your friends and acquaintances consider you to be sophisticated, or whether you have an appreciation for better things, are irrelevant. Your value is the same in both cases.

· Anything or anyone other than you: Here's where we get to the crux of the issue: only you can judge your own value. You are deserving and valued if you believe that to be the case. Guess what, even if you don't think you are deserving and worthwhile, you still are!

Examples of Healthy Self-Worth

Okay, I know what determines self-worth and what doesn't (and shouldn't), but what does healthy self-worth actually entail?

Let's read over a few examples in light of what we know about the factors that affect our sense of self-worth.

Bill performs poorly at school. Even though he studies a lot, he typically receives Bs and Cs. He didn't do well on the SATs, and no one would consider him to be a mathematician. He is also an ordinary reader and struggles to write.

And finally, think about Marcus' situation. Marcus is a great salesman and regularly outsells the majority of the other employees at his company,

And finally, think about Marcus' situation. Marcus is a great salesman and regularly outsells the majority of the other employees at his company, but one colleague always appears to be a little bit in front of him. He enjoys playing squash and participates in competitions frequently. He occasionally comes in first or second, but most of the time he doesn't place at all.Marcus believes that he is valuable even though he is not the best in his career or his favorite activity. Even if he is not the smartest, most talented, or most successful person, he believes that he is intelligent, talented, and successful and is good with it.

How to build self-worth in adolescents

As with most lifelong traits, it's best to start early. If you know any adolescents, be sure to encourage them to understand and accept their own self-worth. Reinforce their value as a being rather than a "doing," as some say—in other words, make sure they know that they are valuable for who they are, not what they do.

How to increase self-worth and self-value in adults

Adults are a little more difficult to develop self-worth and self-value in, but it's still not impossible. To find out how to do it, look at the two suggestions below.

First, review the list of factors that do not affect one's sense of worth. Remind yourself that your worth as a person has nothing to do with your bank account, job title, physical attractiveness, or social media following.

Make an effort to step back and consider what truly matters when determining a person's worth: their kindness, compassion, empathy, respect for others, and how they treat others. It's easy to get caught up in chasing money, status, and popularity—especially when these things are highly valued by those around us and by society as a whole.

However, make an effort to stand back and consider what actually counts when judging a person's value: their kindness, compassion, empathy, respect for others, and how well they treat those around them.

Work on recognising, confronting, and externalising your inner critic. Each of us has an inner critic who enjoys picking apart and pointing out our shortcomings (Firestone, 2014). It's OK to occasionally let our inner critic triumph, but if we do it too frequently, she learns to believe she's correct!

Make your inner critic pause whenever you notice her starting to spew her criticisms.

Consider whether she is being polite, whether her claims are supported by any evidence, and whether you actually need to know what she is telling you. Please feel free to advise her to see herself out if none of those things are true.

Remind her that no matter what you do or don't do, you are still worthwhile and precious by challenging her on the things she whispers in your ear.

See the exercises, activities, and worksheets we discuss later in this article for additional specific activities and suggestions.

One of the biggest mistakes you'll see people with poor self-esteem do is putting all of their value in one area of their lives, which is frequently a relationship.

You are not defined by the affection of another person, and neither is your worth as a person. You are deserving of love and respect whether you are single, casually dating, in a committed relationship, or celebrating your 30th wedding anniversary with your spouse. You should schedule some time to work on your self-acceptance and self-compassion.

Although it applies to everyone, married or not, individuals who are devoted to a relationship may find it to be more important.

Don't fall into the trap of believing that receiving love from your lover qualifies you for love. You don't want to be left with no choice but to start again if your relationship or spouse should suffer any sort of loss. Breakups and grieving may become considerably more difficult than necessary as a result.

You should work on improving your sense of worth because it will also improve your current relationship, even though this aspect of the problem may be enough to motivate you.

You can love someone else more effectively if you can learn to love yourself. Because they are aware that finding their own worth, esteem, and happiness comes first, people with high levels of self-respect tend to have more fulfilling, caring, and stable relationships than those who do not.

Two people who are genuinely happy and confident in themselves shine considerably brighter than two people who are attempting to absorb each other's light .

The Risks of Tying Your Self-Worth to Your Job

There are significant risks associated with connecting your self-worth to your employment, just like the risks associated with anchoring your self-worth to someone else. Jobs can come and go, sometimes without warning, much like a significant other.

You might be shrunk, redirected, released, downsized again, laid off, transferred, dehired, terminated, replaced, asked to resign, or just plain fired. You might also receive new duties and responsibilities that don't align with the sense of worth your former duties and obligations gave you, or you might be transferred, promoted, degraded, or given those tasks.

You may also change jobs, retire, take a break from work, or take a new position—all of which can be fantastic life changes but can become excessively challenging if you place an excessive amount of value on your employment.

As noted earlier, your job is one of the things that don't define you or your worth. There's nothing wrong with being proud of what you do, finding joy or fulfillment in it, or letting it shape who you are; the danger is in letting it define your entire sense of self.

We are all so much more than a job. Believing that we are nothing more than a job is detrimental to our wellbeing and can be disastrous in times of crisis.

Develop your self-awareness

Building self-understanding is a crucial step on the path to self-worth. Before you can conclude that you are a worthy human being, you must first discover who you are and what you want.

There are few simple thought experiment to work on increasing your understanding of yourself:

1. Visualize losing all you own, including your goods, connections, friendships, position in society, career, achievements, etc.

2. Ask yourself the following questions:

1. a. What if all I own were to vanish overnight?
2. b. What if I was the only person left?
3. c. How would I feel if that happened?
4. d. What do I genuinely possess that is valuable?
5. 3. Consider your responses to these queries and see if you can reach the following conclusion: "I'm not affected internally no matter what occurs externally or what is taken away from me"
6. Next, get to know yourself on a deeper level with these questions:
   a. Who I am? I am . . . I am not .
   b. How am I?
   c. How am I in the world?
   d. How do others see me?
   e. How do others speak about me?
   f. What key life moments define who I am today?

g. What brings me the most passion, fulfillment, and joy?

7. Once you have a good understanding of who you are and what fulfills and satisfies you, it's time to look at what isn't so great or easy about being you. Ask yourself these questions:
   a. Where do I struggle most?
   b. Where do I need to improve?
   c. What fears often hold me back?
   d. What habitual emotions hurt me?
   e. What mistakes do I tend to make?
   f. Where do I tend to consistently let myself down?

Finally, take a moment to look at the flipside; ask yourself:

a. What abilities do I have?
b. What am I really good at?

<u>Boost your self-acceptance</u>

The next phase is to improve your acceptance of who you are once you have a clearer understanding of who you are.

Let's start by extending forgiveness to ourselves for anything from item 5 above. Consider any difficulties, areas where you need to grow, errors, and bad habits you may have, and make a commitment to accepting and forgiving yourself without condemnation or justifications.

Repeating the following statements while reflecting on all you discovered about yourself in the first exercise:

I totally accept every aspect of myself, including my flaws, fears, behaviours, and things I might not be too proud of; 1. I accept the good, the bad, and the ugly

I accept who I am and how I am at this moment.

Enhance your self-love

You can start to develop love and care for yourself once you have worked on embracing yourself for who you are. Make it a point to show yourself compassion, kindness, tolerance, and generosity.

Start focusing on the tone you use with yourself to increase self-love. Make a commitment to speaking to yourself more upliftingly and positively.

If you're unsure of where to begin, ponder (or speak aloud) these straightforward statements:

1. I feel loved and special.
2. I genuinely adore myself.
3. I am a deserving and competent individual.
4. Be aware of your value.

You will get at a time where you no longer rely on other people, your accomplishments, or other external sources for your sense of self-worth once you have come to understand, accept, and love yourself.

The best thing you can do at this point is continue to maintain your self-understanding, self-acceptance, self-love, and self-worth. Also, acknowledge your value and thank yourself for the effort you've done to get here.

To affirm your self-worth, keep in mind that:

1. You no longer need to appease others;
2. You alone control how you feel about yourself, regardless of what others do or say or what occurs outside of you; and
3. Your genuine value comes from within, from an internal standard that you have set for yourself.
4. You have the power to react to situations and occurrences using your internal sources, resources, and resourcefulness.
5. Take responsibility for yourself

In this stage, you will practice being responsible for yourself, your circumstances, and your problems.

Follow these guidelines to ensure you are working on this exercise in a healthy way:

- Accept full responsibility for all that occurs without abdicating your own agency;
- Recognize that you have the power to modify and affect the conditions and events in your life.

Remind yourself of the lessons you've learned by completing all of these activities, and keep in mind that you are the one who controls your life. Take pride in your earned feeling of value and work to keep it.

5

Own up your mistakes

Being able to admit your errors is a sign of leadership.

Because nobody is perfect, you will occasionally make mistakes. They can, however, help you develop into a more regarded, trustworthy, and resourceful worker if you own up to them and take the proper corrective action.

An error is an error. Greater trust, respect, and appreciation for you as a leader may come through the process of managing the error. Like anything else, the key is in how you approach it.

As a leader, taking responsibility for your error gives you a crucial sense of security and increases the credibility of your statements. Employees focus their talents and efforts into supporting the leader rather than defending their status inside the company when they feel comfortable. This fosters a culture where employees feel free to take significant risks and own their failures.

It is not at all a strength, but a weakness, and in a leader, it is shortsighted and dangerous, to be unable to see and confess mistakes.

Nobody likes making mistakes, and Psychology Today notes that we occasionally take full responsibility for errors and occasionally just accept partial blame, but it is distinct from a desire to "push back against the actual facts."

Psychological rigidity occurs when someone consistently rejects all facts and is unable to accept that they are mistaken.

Some people have such weak "psychological constitutions," fragile egos, and low self-esteem that it would be too threatening for them to accept admitting they were wrong or made a mistake.

To face the reality and accept responsibility for our errors requires a certain amount of emotional fortitude.

It's a sign that someone's ego is too fragile to allow for the humility (or humanity) of erring if they refuse to acknowledge a mistake in the face of overwhelming evidence, have to shift the blame, deny it, or change the narrative. That goes against leadership.

On a smaller scale, failing to admit a mistake or downplaying it can reveal a lack of understanding of the benefits of doing so for future advancement.

"As any great leader would admit, they have had their share of learning experiences. They'll admit that their collective realization as a result of their mistakes taught them priceless lessons, including how to identify possibilities everywhere and anticipate the unexpected more swiftly.

6

FORGIVE YOURSELF

> "There are only 2 two ways to have a peaceful conscience: Never do anything wrong or learn self-forgiveness (Pro tip: first way's impossible)"
>
> - Elizabeth Gilbert.

A common definition of forgiveness is the conscious choice to release sentiments of rage, resentment, and retaliation toward someone who you feel has wronged you, or even if it is you. Although you could be quite forgiving of others, you might be much more harsh with yourself. Since we have all made mistakes or wished our actions had produced better results, learning to forgive ourselves is essential to moving on.

Everyone makes mistakes, but it's crucial for mental health and wellbeing to learn how to take responsibility for them, move past them, and forgive yourself.

Self-forgiveness is neither a way to absolve oneself of responsibility or a show of fragility. the forgiveness action,

No matter who you are forgiving—whether it is yourself or someone else—you are not necessarily endorsing the behaviour.

It is a tool that helps us confront the things we've done in the past, own our errors, and move on. It does not imply that you approve of or justify what occurred. It doesn't imply that you have forgotten. There is a time for our pain and sorrow. We must possess that. However, the season ends, and life goes on. And we must continue with it.

It's critical to forgive yourself because, if you don't, these incorrect behavior may alter who you are.

It's a frequent notion that refusing to forgive oneself shows you're more sorry; nevertheless, all it does is prevent you from moving forward. We may believe that seeing the world through the worst act we have committed gives us more grace, but this is untrue. In fact, it makes us put ourselves down when we start a relationship. More crucially, choosing to live a less happy life truly means deciding not to forgive yourself.

So how can you learn to forgive yourself if it is such a crucial skill?

- Compassion for oneself. Because life is imperfect, why should humans be? People who practice self-compassion remember this when things are difficult and do not go as planned. They are kind and compassionate to themselves and accept that imperfections are inevitable.
- A common humanity. Everybody encounters obstacles in life. Everyone will experience tough feelings or need to solve problems as unforeseen circumstances happen. Having compassion for yourself entails letting go of the notion that you are the only person in the world to go through these things.

· Focus and awareness. People may feel uneasy while they are experiencing bad feelings. They frequently exaggerate or minimise these feelings. Self-compassion is demonstrated by the ability to calmly sit with these emotions and recognize them for what they are.

Self-forgiveness is a means of reconciling the way you view yourself after you have felt guilt, humiliation, and disappointment, although self-compassion is not. When you do anything that causes you to doubt your perception of yourself, these emotions appear. It is a component of self-compassion as a result.

Strategies for Self-Forgiveness

- You might occasionally act in a way that contradicts your perception of yourself. And when you act in a way that hurts you or someone else, it can be challenging to come to terms with yourself. Here are some suggestions for internal self-forgiveness exercises:

· Reflect back. Consider a period in your life when you experienced safety and compassion. Keep in mind who that person is; it might be a friend, relative, mentor, teacher, spiritual leader, or even a pet. Imagine yourself feeling safe and secure around them. Be able to feel secure. then, along with

- your protector, list all of your positive qualities.
- · Recall the occasion. The next step is to accept the truth about the things you need to forgive yourself for. Think back to the particular incident and the emotions it evoked. Note what it is difficult to face. Make a list of everything that occurred and divide it into three categories: moral failings, incompetence, and other.

Moral failings call for regret or guilt, whereas incompetence calls for repentance, such as pledging never to repeat a certain action.

- • Resist avoiding guilt. It's normal and good to feel awful about doing something bad. What remains after we eliminate the negative emotions brought on by wrongdoing? Shame and guilt are not the same thing, though. Shame is accompanied by retaliatory emotions like denial, avoidance, and violence.
- • Telling yourself that you are fundamentally a bad person and feel guilty is not helpful. You might not believe that you can change as a result. But feeling bad about your behaviour can motivate you to avoid doing it again.

• Assume accountability. If you don't take responsibility for what you did, both to yourself and to the person you wronged, it's impossible to forgive yourself. •Let them and yourself know that you accept responsibility for what you did. Learn to accept yourself completely for what you did.

Make an effort to fix the harm. If you believe you haven't taken the necessary steps to make amends, it could be difficult for you to genuinely forgive yourself.

• Feel sympathy for people other than oneself. People have been observed to struggle with self

forgiveness when they also feel sympathy for the other party. It's common for folks to experience stress like this. However, this self-forgiveness can be hollow and have little meaning if you don't have empathy for both yourself and the other person.

Implementing these suggestions can be challenging, but so can practising genuine self-forgiveness. It will probably be a protracted voyage with peaks and dips. You might never be able to entirely let go of your bad emotions. Self-forgiveness doesn't have to be indulgent; rather, it should be an honest assessment of your capacity for both good and terrible deeds.

9 798888 331767

Printed by Libri Plureos GmbH in Hamburg, Germany